LETS
GO
PUBLISH!

iv

Rush Limbaugh's Platform for Americans

Platform points Rush would endorse if he ran for President!

If Rush Limbaugh were my next-door neighbor, I would still listen to him on the radio every day from 12 to 3 unless he was on TV. I listen every day as he gets through all the clutter of the day better and quicker than anybody else on radio or TV. He is the best, period.

Nobody can be anybody else but there are times I think exactly like Rush. So, now that I have developed a few sure-fire solutions to immigration, I figure he is with me and so I titled the book accordingly.

Running for office is a grueling, tiring, busy, and difficult process. There is always something to do. There is always someone who wants something from you. and did I say you are always tired. Yet, somehow, you have to walk around with a smile on your face and a nice comment ready to come from your lips even if it is a bad day. Even if your purpose for running is altruistic so you can help your city, state, or the country, and you really do not want to be a politician, just a worthy representative of the people, there are many who simply will not believe you.

So, here I am with the only idea in the world that actually solves the problem with illegal interlopers hiding in the shadows of the United States. Moreover, the platform addresses Obamacare, Millennials, and Senior Citizens. It is designed with something good for everybody

The real concern many conservatives have is whether any political party is interested in a solution as they seem content to having no solution as their solution. Democrats want everybody to vote and Republicans want the cheapest labor possible. The bulk of American, when polled want neither. They want a country that is all-American with Americans in the driver's seat; and they want their guests to be invited to the table.

You won't want to put this book down as you learn the ins & outs of how there really is a solution that Rush will like. That's more than enough for me. How about you?

ii

Copyright © August 2018, Brian W. Kelly; ....Editor: Brian P. Kelly
Title: Rush Limbaugh's Platform for Americans   Author Brian W. Kelly
Platform points Rush would endorse if he ran for President!

Published by: .... LETS GO PUBLISH!
Editor in Chief..Brian P. Kelly
Email: .... info@letsgopublish.com
Web site..www.letsgopublish.com

Library of Congress Copyright Information Pending
Book Cover Design by Brian W. Kelly

Text Editor—Brian P. Kelly

ISBN Information: The International Standard Book Number (ISBN) is a unique machine-readable identification number, which marks any book unmistakably. The ISBN is the clear standard in the book industry. 159 countries and territories are officially ISBN members. The Official ISBN for this book is

978-1-947402-50-8

The price for this work is.............. .... $6.95 USD

10	9	8	7	6	5	4	3	2	1

Release Date: .... August 2018

Dedication

I dedicate this book to my wonderful wife Patricia; our three wonderful children Brian, Mike and Katie; and our friendly friends—Ben our always very happy dog, who recently became an Angel, and Buddy, our always cheerful Catholic cat.

Thank You All!

Acknowledgments

I appreciate all the help that I have received in putting this book together as well as all of my other 164 other published books.

My printed acknowledgments had become so large that book readers "complained" about going through too many pages to get to page one of the text.

And, so to permit me more flexibility, I put my acknowledgment list online, and it continues to grow. Believe it or not, it once cost about a dollar more to print each book.

Thank you and God bless you all for your help.

Please check out www.letsgopublish.com to read the latest version of my heartfelt acknowledgments updated for this book. FYI, Wily Ky Eyely, my wonderful basketball playing "niece," loves this book and recommends it to all. She wants "Uncle Brian" to be our next US Senator.

Click the bottom of the Main menu to see the big acknowledgments!

Thank you all!

Preface

Why did Brian W. Kelly write this book?

Brian W. Kelly loves America and he developed a number of unique approaches to solving some major issues in America. Pennsylvanians suffer from these as much as those from other states. Four times Brian Kelly has run for public office. Twice he went through the ballot access process as he ran for Congress in Northeastern PA and he ran for Mayor in his home town of Wilkes-Barre, PA.

Two other times, including 2018, Kelly ran for the US Senate as a write-in candidate. The cost in time and money for a regular person to achieve 2000 nomination petition signatures and travel around the state of Pennsylvania is far too prohibitive for the common man. Sometimes getting one's platform exposed to the public is reward enough when the full goal is unachievable.

Brian Kelly gets much of his message out in the books that he writes. This book is Brian's 167th of 165 non-fiction books. It is about four important solutions, two of which are not yet on the top ten list for all Americans. But they will be as soon as the people understand fully how the solutions benefit America and Americans.

Rush Limbaugh is a man, who spends his days behind an EIB microphone and during these days, he is known better than the great Clark Kent, a mild-mannered reporter for a great metropolitan newspaper, as he instructs Americans about how to deal with the events of the day.

However, most of us, who know him well from hearing his knowledgeable and powerful voice every day, see him and his alter ego as the same—one who does not work on the Rush Limbaugh show or the Daily Planet. His alter ego as we all know came to Earth with powers and abilities far beyond those of mortal men. We have seen him change the course of mighty rivers, bend steel in his bare hands, and disguised as Rush Limbaugh, this Superman fights a never-ending battle for truth, justice, and the American way with a 99% accuracy rating. And, nobody cares about that 1%.

Rush Limbaugh is not running for President, but he would make a great one. So, this is not his platform and he did not develop it. It was developed by your author and it is so good that Rush as Rush, Clarke or Superman would surely endorse it because it is good for America and Americans.

I hope you enjoy this book and I hope that it inspires you to consider the platforms presented as enabling the greatness of America. Americans must

take the individual actions necessary to help the government of the US
refrain from fraudulent abuse of seniors and millennials in addition to
putting all Americans before all foreign interlopers.

Brian W. Kelly has the solutions for America and the Kelly Team is in
accord that Rush Limbaugh will help Kelly and all those on the team to do
what is best to move America closer to its greatness destination.

I wish you the best.

Brian P. Kelly, Publisher
Wilkes-Barre, Pennsylvania

Table of Contents

About the Author

Brian W. Kelly retired as an Assistant Professor in the Business Information Technology (BIT) program at Marywood University, where he also served as the IBM i and Midrange Systems Technical Advisor to the IT Faculty. Kelly designed, developed, and taught many college and professional courses. He continues as a contributing technical editor to a number of IT industry magazines, including "The Four Hundred" and "Four Hundred Guru," published by IT Jungle.

Kelly is a former IBM Senior Systems Engineer and IBM Mid Atlantic Area Specialist. His specialty was designing applications for customers as well as implementing advanced IBM operating systems and software facilities on their machines.

He has an active information technology consultancy. He is the author of 167 books and numerous technical articles. Kelly has been a frequent speaker at COMMON, IBM conferences, and other technical conferences.

Brian was a candidate for US Congress from Pennsylvania in 2010 and he brings a lot of experience to his writing endeavors. Brian is ready to be your Senator in 2019. Through this book, Brian Kelly asks Rush Limbaugh for his assistance in getting the word out on his candidacy and his unique platform.

Chapter 1 Who is Rush Limbaugh?

Rush would say that he is the Doctor of Democracy?

The biographical facts on Rush Limbaugh are taken from his web site at the following link: https://www.rushlimbaugh.com/americas-anchorman. There are some personal opinions and the opinions of fans and foes mixed in this chapter to give a more complete picture of the man we can rightfully call, the Superman of the Airwaves.

Rush Limbaugh does appear to be more Superman than Clark Kent to his legion of followers / fans. There is not much not to like. That elusive 1% that leaves him with a 99% accuracy rating is the only negative I can think of and to his legions, this means absolutely nothing.

He is worth every penny he makes. I am sure he spends it well, but I do have one major wish as to how I would spend some of Mr. Limbaugh net worth and his salary / proceeds if I were enabled to do so. I would like Mr. Limbaugh to form a consortium with some other conservative talk show personalities who have done well in life, and together, I would like to see them buy a TV Network to help even the score against the Fake News Media.

At 67 years of age, Rush Limbaugh is worth a cool **$500 Million**. Rush Hudson Limbaugh III earned it all the hard way—the American way, through his own genius.

Limbaugh sees himself as an American entertainer, radio talk show host, writer, conservative political commentator, and media personality. I see him as a valuable asset who remains vigilant to the needs of America and the subversive efforts of the drive-by media to make America small.

In his efforts, he has become the most popular radio host in America and when he was on TV, most of his legions, such as me, were ardent watchers and supporters of his video efforts. He tried his luck as a part-time NFL football commentator, but he learned that the truth is not always a welcome attribute to liberal media outlets such as ESPN. In fact, we can say the same about the liberal "I stand for the National Anthem" National Football League." They were happy to remove Rush from their left-wing broadcast team.

Limbaugh currently resides in Palm Beach, Florida, where he also broadcasts The Rush Limbaugh Show. According to December 2015 estimates by Talkers Magazine, Rush Limbaugh has an audience of 26 million right now, which is the highest ever for the program. As the antidote for fake news, Limbaugh's program is right on the mark and the people love it and reward him by faithful listening.

After Trump's election in 2016, the Rush audience continued to grow even though the election was over, and the people had made their choice for President. All aspects of the Limbaugh connection are growing such as his Rush Revers book series, Subscribers at Rush 24/7, and Subscribers at the Limbaugh Letter. Everything is pointing upwards as sales continue to grow.

Rush says that on a program such as his, when you have an intense election that features a campaign of a minimum one year or longer, once that election is finished, and the results are in, the intensity usually lightens and fades away and the audience gets interested in things that they have been putting off. However, this did not happen in 2016. His audience continued to build and quite frankly, we who depend on Rush to sort it all out, are very happy about that.

When Rush recently reported his listening statistics, it was a reinforcement, like a validation. He noted that ratings are taken now constantly. It used to be they were taken four times a year. Rush recently commented that "Now they're [ratings] taken constantly. They fluctuate depending on a lot of factors, if I don't mind saying so myself. And I just happened to mention it in passing and got this gratified thank-you email note, so I wanted to repeat that."

Since Rush Limbaugh was 16 years old, he has been intrigued with radio jobs, He worked a series of disc jockey jobs right from the start. He began his talk show back in 1984 at Sacramento, California radio station KFBK. It featured the typical Limbaugh format of political commentary and listener calls. In 1988, Limbaugh moved it all to New York and began broadcasting his show nationally from radio station WABC in New York City. The show's flagship station became WOR in 2014.

In the 1990s, Limbaugh's first books *The Way Things Ought to Be* (1992) and *See, I Told You So* (1993) made The New York Times Best Seller list. In his books and on his show, Rush Limbaugh frequently criticizes what he regards as liberal policies and politicians, as well as what he perceives as a pervasive liberal bias in major U.S. media. Trump calls it fake news. Limbaugh calls it liberal bias.

Mr. Limbaugh gets paid a zillion dollars for what he does, and he is worth it. He is among the highest-paid people in U.S. media, signing a contract in 2008 for $400 million through 2016. In 2017, Forbes listed his earnings at $84 million for the previous 12 months and ranked him the 11th highest-earning celebrity in the world. His most recent contract, signed on July 31, 2016, will take his radio program to 2020, its 32nd year. It would be tough for the world of truth and goodness to have to live without Rush Limbaugh. He is as good as it gets in many more ways than one.

On his web site, Mr. Limbaugh loves referring to himself as the "Doctor of Democracy." The Rushmeister, who also likes referring to himself as a harmless lovable little fuzzball, is known as the pioneer of AM radio. It is all true. He admits that he did not invent the radio. He thinks history got it right crediting Italian inventor and engineer Guglielmo Marconi (1874-1937).

Marconi developed, demonstrated and marketed the first successful long-distance wireless telegraph and in 1901 broadcast the first transatlantic radio signal. Limbaugh took Marconi's invention and with it, he beats out most of the TV markets. Rush Limbaugh may be solely responsible for bringing radio back from the graveyard of obsolete devices.

Limbaugh revolutionized the media and political landscape with his unprecedented combination of serious discussion of political, cultural and social issues along with satirical and biting humor, which parodies previously "untouchable" personalities and topics. His passion inspires millions of Americans to be the best they can be, and he continually keeps the country on course to a brighter future.

I recall that in the 1980's I was subject to too many talk show hosts with a liberal progressive bias. It was so unnerving for me, that I would seek out some FM music to get away from the unpleasant din.

Then on August 1, 1988, Rush Limbaugh saved me. He launched his phenomenally successful radio show known as The Rush Limbaugh Show into national syndication with 56 radio stations. Here we are 30 years later, and the show is now heard on more than 600 stations by up to 27 million people each week and is the highest-rated national radio talk show in America.

Rush Limbaugh helps conservatives, nationalists, and populists, understand that it doesn't have to be this way. He got us through the Obama years and now he is reinforcing the idea that most of the news is fake and the objective of the press is to destroy Donald Trump. Because Americans know this for sure thanks to Rush's help, the left is defeated on every attempt to spread their vile fake news often before it leaks out the door.

Rush may not be Marconi, but he was awarded the Marconi Radio Award for "Syndicated Radio Personality of the Year" by the National Association of Broadcasters in 1992, 1995, 2000, 2005, and 2014. He was inducted into the Radio Hall of Fame in 1993, the National Association of Broadcasters Hall of Fame in 1998, and the Hall of Famous Missourians in 2012.

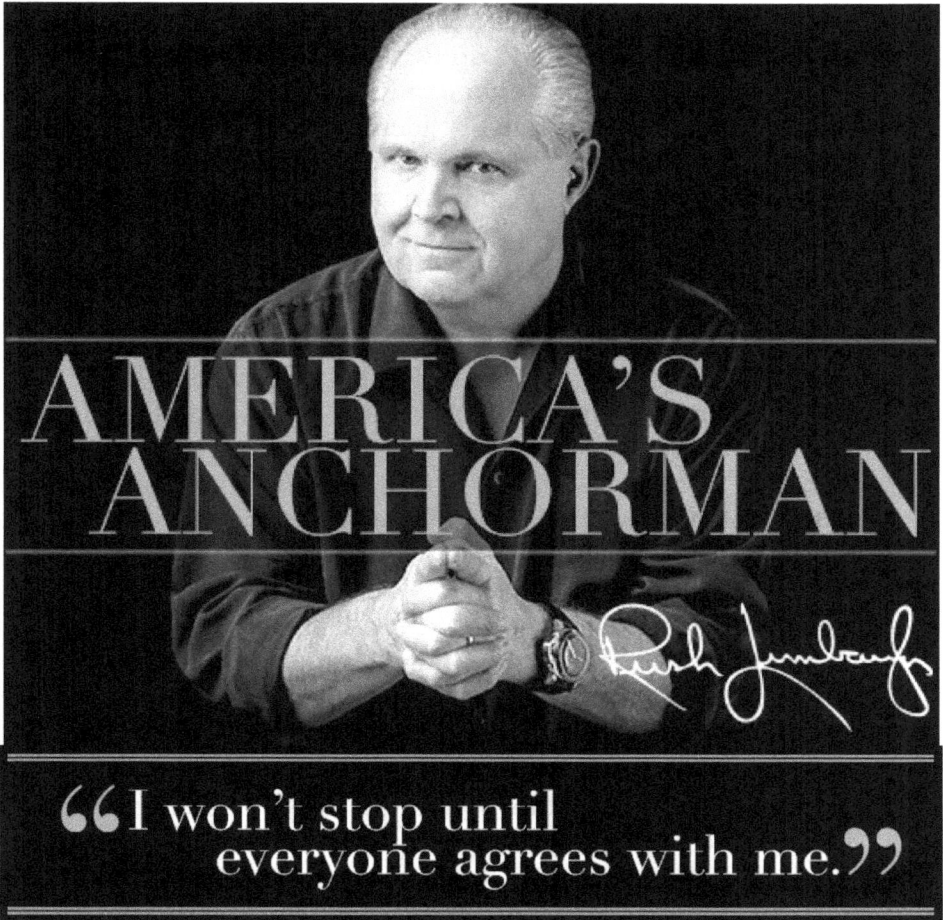

AMERICA'S
ANCHORMAN

❝I won't stop until everyone agrees with me.❞

Even Rush's harshest critics will admit that he has had a distinguished career in radio and TV, even though he had to do it the tough way—hard work. Here is a sampling of his many recognitions. It is long because that's how long Rush has been on America's team and it shows how effective he has been:

✓ Five-time winner of the National Association of Broadcasters Marconi Award for "Excellence in Syndicated and Network Broadcasting"
✓ Children's Choice Author of the Year, Rush Revere and the Brave Pilgrims (2014)

- ✓ Author of #1 New York Times bestselling Adventures of Rush Revere Series, including Rush Revere and the Brave Pilgrims, The First Patriots, The American Revolution, The Star-Spangled Banner, and The Presidency
- ✓ Author of The Limbaugh Letter, the most widely read political newsletter in the country and two #1 New York Times best-selling books, The Way Things Ought to Be and See, I Told You So, which have sold nearly 10 million copies. Additionally, See, I Told You So set an American publishing record
- ✓ Inducted into the Radio Hall of Fame in Chicago in 1993
- ✓ Inducted into the National Association of Broadcasters Hall of Fame in 1998
- ✓ Inducted into the Hall of Famous Missourians on May 14, 2012 at the State Capitol building in Jefferson City
- ✓ Hosted Rush Limbaugh – The Television Show in New York from 1992 through 1996
- ✓ Received a personal letter from President Ronald Reagan thanking him and naming him the "Number One voice for conservatism in our Country"
- ✓ Invited to stay in the Lincoln Bedroom in the White House by President George H. W. Bush
- ✓ Honorary Member of the Republican Freshman Class of 1995 House of Representatives
- ✓ Barbara Walters' 10 Most Fascinating People (2008)
- ✓ Time Magazine's 100 Most Influential People in the World (2009)
- ✓ Forbes Magazine's 50 Most Powerful Celebrities in the United States, numerous years (#19 in 2010)
- ✓ Awarded the "William F. Buckley, Jr. Award for Media Excellence" by the Media Research Center (2007)
- ✓ Received CPAC's "Defender of the Constitution Award" (2009)
- ✓ Named the Human Events Man of the Year (2007)
- ✓ The Giving Back Fund's 10 Most Generous Celebrities for contributions to charities and individuals, such as the Marine Corps – Law Enforcement Foundation
- ✓ Hosted an annual radio Cure-a-thon to benefit research done by the Leukemia & Lymphoma Society (LLS)— raising over $47 million to date

✓ Miss America® Pageant Judge 2010
✓ Guest Television appearances include Nightline with Ted Koppel, Cross Fire™, Good Morning America®, CBS This Morning™, The Today® Show,The Phil Donahue Show™, The Late Show® with David Letterman, The Tonight Show®, This Week™ with David Brinkley, Meet the Press® with Tim Russert, and The Drew Carey Show®. Starred as himself in the popular network sitcoms Family Guy® and Hearts Afire®
✓ Profiled on CBS's 60 Minutes®, ABC's 20/20® and in numerous publications including U.S. News and World Report®, Newsweek®, National Review™, Time Magazine®, The New York Times® Magazine and USA Weekend®

Let's quickly review the bio from when Rush was a baby until he became the #1 man in radio.

Rush Limbaugh was born the son of Mildred Carolyn "Millie" (née Armstrong) and Rush Hudson Limbaugh Jr. His father was a lawyer and a U.S. fighter pilot who served in the China Burma India Theater of World War II. Mrs. Limbaugh was from Searcy, Arkansas. The unique name "Rush" was originally chosen for his grandfather to honor the maiden name of family member, Edna Rush.

With a full name of Rush Hudson Limbaugh III, the stork presented a major gift to the Limbaugh family in 1951. The Limbaugh's as a family were part of a long line of attorneys. But not Rush. He did not like school, but he did know what he liked. At 16, he chose to explore his passion for broadcasting by working as a disc jockey for a hometown radio station.

After four years, he left for Pittsburgh to work for the former ABC owned and operated KQV. Tired of the disc jockey life, Rush briefly left broadcasting for business, joining the Kansas City Royals as Director of Group Sales, and later as Director of Sales and Special Events. He fondly remembers his days with Kansas City and his relationship with some of their stellar players such as George Brett.

Rush couldn't resist the urge to return to broadcasting. In 1983, he re-entered radio as a political commentator for KMBZ in Kansas City. A year later Rush hosted a daytime talk show in Sacramento, California, tripling the program's ratings in four years. From there, in 1988, he went on to New York where the record-breaking national show was born.

Chapter 2 Elect Brian Kelly as Your Senator from PA.

About you

When you decide that a political career is for you, make sure you highlight your finest points. If you were Brian Kelly, this might be some of what you would say. This is what Brian Kelly says about himself as he puts together his campaign buzz for US Senator.

Brian Kelly is married to the former Patricia Piotroski, and the couple resides in Northeastern Pennsylvania as they have all their married life of forty-one years. They are the proud parents of three wonderful adult children, Brian, Michael, and Katie. Ben, the family canine, and Buddy, the family feline, reside with Pat and Brian, but are loved by all.

Brian Kelly was born and "raised" in Wilkes-Barre PA. He attended St. Boniface Grade School and Meyers High School. Brian was both a pitcher and a catcher on the Meyers High Baseball team and he was active in many school clubs as well as the student council.

Brian competed for an academic scholarship to King's College and was awarded a four-year academic scholarship grant, a National Defense Student Loan, and a work-study job. The job in the federal work-study program helped him make up a $50.00 per year tuition shortfall.

Tuition was $475.00 per semester. Scholarship was $250, and loan was $200. Brian is most grateful to King's College for the Academic scholarship and to the Federal Government for the loan and work-study assistance. His degree was the difference between a successful business life and a blue-collar job.

Brian graduated cum laude ranked #29 of 382 from King's with a degree in Data Processing, the pre-cursor degree to Business Information Technology. While at King's, Kelly was a member of two honor societies, the King's Aquinas Society, and the Delta Epsilon Sigma National Honor Society. Brian played varsity Baseball for the Monarchs as a catcher / pinch hitter, and then as a starting pitcher in his Junior and Senior years.

After King's, he joined the IBM Corporation as a Computer Science Systems Assistant where he spent 23 years before retiring, under a special program, as a Senior Systems Engineer. During his IBM career, Kelly received his M.B.A. summa cum laude in Accounting and Finance from Wilkes University. After his time at IBM, Brian accepted a position with College Misericordia as its Chief Technology Director / Internal IT Consultant. At the same time, he initiated his own IT Consulting Practice, Kelly Consulting.

After building the College Misericordia campus network, its connection to the Internet, its email and its Web servers, Kelly left College Misericordia and moved on to spend full time in his own IT business consulting practice. In 2004, Kelly joined the faculty of Marywood University and, in addition to maintaining his consulting practice, Brian served Marywood as an Assistant Professor of Business Information Technology and as its IBM i system technology assistant to the Business Information Technology Faculty.

Contact campaign@yourwebsite.com

An Entreaty to vote for Brian Kelly

Fellow Citizens of Northeastern Pennsylvania, I would like to present myself as a Candidate to be your US Senator for the State of Pennsylvania. As you know, this seat is currently held by Bob Casey Jr. but not for long. I am running as a write-in candidate, a Democrat against Mr. Casey in the General Election on November 6, 2018.

If I don't make it, my backup is Lou Barletta a great Congressman who is supported in 2018's general election for US Senator by President Donald Trump. The President came to the Wilkes-Barre Pa area to support Barletta the first week of August 2018.

I am proud to say that--but for a few years as an independent living in Utica, NY, I would be a lifetime Democrat and a lifetime resident of Northeastern PA. Right after I earned my Bachelor of Science from King's College at the age of 21, I competed in a tough job marketplace, and I had the good fortune of being hired to work as a Systems Engineer at IBM in Utica, New York. For two years, I lived in Utica as a registered Independent.

My dad, a lifetime Democrat, was very conservative and good man. He was a staunch believer in the importance of labor unions to help the working man in America. He worked as heating specialist at R. A. Davis in Wilkes-Barre and then as laborer at Stegmaier Brewery on "Brewery Hill" in Wilkes-Barre for thirty-one years until the Stegmaier label was purchased by the Lion Incorporated. At that time, the Lion proudly brewed Gibbons Beer.

[G-I-B-B-O-N-S, pure refreshing Gibbons. If it's Gibbons, it's good—so the next time you should say gimme Gibbons!]

That is the essence of the 1960's Gibbons commercial.

Stegmaier of course brewed a number of different beers, including Stegmaier Beer, Ale, Porter, and Bach. When I was in my twenties, the "Brewery" brought back Liebotschaner, a finely crafted and aged old-time Stegmaier formulation. The company made its beer from fresh grains and hops and malt and it aged all of its products in huge vats on the left side of Market St. as one headed up Brewery Hill.

[So! If you want a beer that's mellow, a beer that is really grand, say hey, make mine Stegmaier, the gold medal beer of the land. And, so at home, or club, or tap room; always order the beer that they cheer. Served just right; mellow, cool, and light, Stegmaier Gold Medal Beer.]

The paragraph above is the essence of the 1960's Stegmaier commercial.

My dad was pretty good at what he did, and he took his work seriously. For a number of years before its demise, Stegmaier had one of the fastest canning machines in Pennsylvania. My dad operated this behemoth single-handedly. For its day, it was an awesome machine. It put out 600 cans per minute. That's even fast according to today's standards. My dad was quite a guy.

My father and I regularly had discussions about beliefs and ideologies and which candidate truly was best for official jobs, at the local, state, and federal levels. More often than not, he and I were on the same page. My dad's philosophy was that you should always vote for the best candidate for the job, not simply the political party. These discussions eventually prompted me to cancel my registration as an independent and become a Democrat. In Pennsylvania, Independents have no voice in the primary elections.

Lots of discontent is not only brewing; it's boiling-over.

There is a storm of discontent content brewing across the United States. You can feel it wherever you go. Regular Americans are beginning to pay attention to what our Congressional representatives have been doing against our will in Washington, D.C. Politics and government, and their collective effect on what's happening in America have become regular dinner table topics.

I know few people today who think President Obama was a good president. In fact, most of my friends have him slotted as one of the worst presidents ever. I think they are right! Sometimes particular Democrats do not have it right. It is OK to be upset. It is OK to show some disgust for what these knaves such as Bob Casey Jr. have done to

America. It's OK to be disgusted, Me too! That's why I am running for the US Senate.

I am still a Democrat because like you I am hoping it becomes a party that mirrors the people rather than going so far left we are all left behind. The leaders of the Democratic Party have betrayed the common man, such as you and me; but none of us writing or reading this paragraph are dead and so we can change the Democratic Party, so it no longer is a party of identity politics that separates Americans under the guise of diversity. Instead for the sake of American unity, we can all join together under the huge umbrella of the US Constitution and reject those leaders who have led us down a path to perdition.

What's not OK is to sit around and let these same elitist establishment types come back again in 2019 to inflict more harm on the American people. Vote them out. You have the power! We have the power!

I decided to run for the US Senate as a write-in candidate because somebody has to represent US. I am a write-in because it means that I do not have to bootlick the rich and powerful for donations. We need change more now than when we thought we needed change and brought in Obama. God gave us Donald Trump as a model for how things should be done.

What we do not need is the kind of change that exalts one man and attempts to silence a nation. I ask you to vote "for the people" on November 6 of this year. Vote out the proponents of big, intrusive, freedom-taking government and all the politicians will disappear overnight.

It seems the kind of change we have been getting from our former anti-American President and the corrupt Congress was good only for the government and the high-paid bureaucrats. It is not the right formula for freedom-loving Americans. While you and I are asking to have government less involved in our daily lives, Congress and our former president were throwing one freedom-stealing regulation after another on us on their way to making this a socialist nation. This Congress does not represent the people.

We can fix that. All we have to do is vote them out. The people think that they are powerless, yet we have all the power. I am running for the US Senate and I am a Democrat. Please do not vote for anybody who has hurt Donald Trump's presidency in the general election.

Don't count on other states to get this job done without our participation. It all starts at home. For US, that is Pennsylvania. Our time has come. Good-by to all the incumbents who are contributing to the downfall of America. Good-by to Bob Casey, an embarrassment to Northeastern PA. Hold your collective noses and then vote him out!

I would hope that by learning about who I am and where I am from and what I stand for, you will conclude that we have unity of purpose. I am one of the regular people in life. I believe that it is my time to serve and if you will permit me, I would be honored to be your Senator for all the regular people in Pennsylvania.

Things worth repeating are worth repeating

Here is some stuff from a press release by the campaign that is very readable and as are most of Brian Kelly's writings. It calls the people to action. Brian believes that we the people have no choice than to be more than mere passers-by in a country being dragged into submission by people who hate America.

*** PRESS RELEASE ***
BRIAN KELLY ANNOUNCES HIS CANDIDACY FOR the US SENATE FROM PENNSYLVAMIA.

Kelly Says It Is Time to Return the Government to The People!

Brian Kelly, a former IBM Senior Systems Engineer and Assistant Professor of Business and Information Technology (BIT) at Marywood University in Scranton, announced his write-in candidacy for the US Senate .

Kelly has promised that he will run as an independent write-in candidate as a Democrat in the general election since he did not compete in the primary election. Brian asks all Democrats to vote for him in the general election as he will serve all voters well.

Brian Kelly has worked in the private sector all his life. He hates what is happening to the US and to Pennsylvania and his solutions are designed to make it better.

Brian Kelly expresses his reason for running for public office in these simple terms: "to return our government back to the people." Kelly notes that government spending is out of control and that only a change in leadership can turn government away from more unpopular tax-payer funded bailouts, crippling taxes and government-takeovers. Casey, a successful lawyer of course is for more spending and for more taxing of those who earn a living in Pennsylvania.

Brian sees the solution as "We must create jobs, not destroy them. The policies of Bob Casey and Barack Obama were killing US businesses before Donald Trump was elected. Like many, I fear the building of a huge, never ending bureaucracy wherever you look." Brian believes that Bob Casey must go so a Trump-Friendly legislature can be in place to help America.

Kelly finds government as the only "industry" which prospered before Trump. Now, all of America is moving forward, and those who are in the way of the Make America Great Again agenda, both Republicans and Democrats need to be replaced. That's why you need to write-in

B-R-I-A-N K-E-L-L Y.

Brian fears the seemingly predestined government takeover of healthcare, the disrupting of the doctor patient relationships, and the bankrupt notion of repressive energy tax legislation and the destruction of the industry that produces America's most abundant energy source-coal. He is concerned that all of this excessive government, which the incumbent supports, will make it tough for Americans to live like Americans. "You can be assured that I will work to stop these flawed changes brought about by poor leadership." Kelly said.

Kelly said that in order to restore the economy, "a brand-new Congress must be committed to getting government to stop micro-managing the economy." They must support Donald Trump to help America.

Government takeovers, national debt, a huge deficit, and the major job killing regulations of the Obama / Casey administration are being rejected summarily by all Americans.

Pennsylvanians will be hurt even more than others by the shutdown of coal and an "energy tax" since many PA communities still have a viable coal industry. Casey is not for Pennsylvanians and his votes could kill the energy industry in PA through taxes or restrictive regulations.

Besides being unfriendly to Pennsylvania business and industry, the only creators of lasting jobs, Bob Casey is vulnerable in 2018 because his positions mirror those of the unpopular Chuck Schumer, Nancy Pelosi, and Maxine Watters. Why would our Senator, against constituent write-ins, support Obamacare and other socialist, budget busting legislation?

Kelly boasts that he has the backing of no political machine and he is taking no political contributions. "It sure should save a lot of time, not having to run fund-raisers." Kelly said. He is proud to say that his total war chest from contributions is $0.00, and he is nowhere close to having to pay the "Obama / Casey Rich Tax."

Kelly feels his message will be brought forth now that he has made it known that he is a serious contender for the nomination and for election in November 2018. By writing in the name Brian Kelly, the people will recognize that a regular old "John Doe," not a political operative has made himself available to the people.

Kelly once had a lot of affinity for the "Tea Party People," and those like you and I, who are not part of a named group but who nonetheless have been justifiably enraged at the unresponsiveness of our government. From Kelly's perspectives, the left made the tea party seem like a bunch of life perverts and nobody complained loud enough to know they that it was not the tea, it was the name and it was the people, regular people who the left hoped to discredit but could not because they were simply you and me. .

Kelly said: "At this stage of my life, I see things that can be so much better if Americans had better representation. I feel in many ways like George Bailey from the Building and Loan in "It's a Wonderful Life," seeing the face of the corrupt Mr. Potter in too many hallways of government.

"I'd like to take the spirit of WW II Brigadier General Jimmy Stewart (real life) as George Bailey and keep all the Potters out of government for an awful long time--even if it means that I have to put in a few years myself." See Chapter 6 for a perspective on Jimmy Stewart as Mr. Jefferson Smith.

Kelly is not interested in a career in politics and when elected will stay for just one or at most two terms. Kelly says: "A regular person holding an office becomes a politician when trying to be reelected."

When the constituents of Pennsylvania get in the "voting booth," no matter how many dollars Bob Casey has spent to advance his candidacy, the only thing voters must remember is two words forming one name, Brian Kelly. It is just ten letters and a space. When they write that name in BRIAN KELLY on the ballot, things will begin to change almost immediately.

"The voters will ask themselves, 'is he a politician?' and the answer of course is 'no.' As voters across the US are trying to free themselves from machine politics, with votes to the highest bidders, Brian Kelly is betting that in Northeastern PA, being 'of the people' will matter more than anything on November 6, 2019. " Kelly said.

As an author, Brian Kelly wishes he were not so old that he has been able to write 165 books, many of which are in the high-tech field. He is tickled, however, that he has written over sixty books since 2010 hoping to convince his fellow Democrats that we must not permit the power brokers in the Democratic Party to ever win again. We can still be good Democrats if we force the power brokers to be more human.

In 2007, Brian Kelly began research for his first book about government. In 2008, he released these first efforts with a book titled, <u>Taxation Without Representation</u>, sold on the Internet at such places as Amazon.com and Barnes & Noble. He has updated the Taxation book and wrote many new patriotic books since then.

These are the product of major research as well as his clear opinions as to how the country has gotten off course. Two of his newest books include <u>Wilkes-Barre PA Return to Glory!</u> and <u>The Constitution 4 Dummmies, and Millennials are people too !!!</u> . Those who think the thoughts of the people do not matter, will not read any of these books

Kelly is an ardent defender of the Constitution and in many of his books, he adds appendices with the full text of the US Constitution and other founding documents.

By visiting this website at <u>www.kellyforussenate.com</u> or by reading his books, available at amazon.com/author/brianwkelly, it is easy to know that Brian Kelly stands where you stand on the issues of the day. He sounds like one of US because he is one of US.

Brian Kelly asks all Democrats and Republicans in Pennsylvania to write-in Brian Kelly in the General Election on November 6. Two words, both are needed for a valid write-in. "I promise that you will have change --- this time it will be change that you can live with." And, won't that be a grand day. ---------

Best wishes for a better America from Brian Kelly.

Sometimes it helps to see things again in summary form:

Brian Kelly's Summary Background:

- E. L. Meyers High, W-B, PA, with honors
- B. S. from King's College cum laude
- M. B. A. from Wilkes University magna cum laude
- 23 years with IBM Corporation as Senior Systems Engineer
- 15 Year Ongoing Consultancy--Business and IT Consultant
- 5 years Misericordia University, Chief Tech Officer

- 7 years with Marywood University -- Assistant Professor, Business Information technology
- Author—164 books, Hundreds of magazine articles

Brian Kelly believes in the effort to restore reverence for God and respect for the unalienable rights to life and liberty in America.

Brian Kelly believes and understands the notion of self-government of, by, and for the people – as well as our moral, physical, and economic sovereignty. Kelly has written four books in this regard:

Taxation Without Representation; *Obama's Seven Deadly Sins* - ; and Healthcare Accountability. Included in each of the first three books is a full copy of the Constitution of the United States, something that we all should keep in our hands in these trying times. Kelly penned another book titled: Jobs! Jobs! Jobs! in 2010.

Altogether he has written 164 books. Most were penned between 2010 to 2018. All are available from amazon.com/author/brianwkelly

Brian Kelly is easy to understand. He is in synch with the Donald Trump agenda. He is an advocate of a complete overhaul of our taxing system and the abolishment of the 16th Amendment, thereby eliminating the tax code and the IRS. The Fair Tax has many advantages over the current income tax system. The Fair tax seems to have the most advantages of all other options, but even the Flat tax is far better than our current income tax system

- Brian Kelly is an advocate of strong border security
- Brian Kelly is ready to declare our nation's reliance on God as fundamental.
- Brian Kelly will work to protect our unalienable rights to life, liberty, and private property.
- Brian Kelly will help restore and protect our constitutional republican form of government.
- Brian Kelly will work to protect the institution of marriage and the traditional family.
- Brian Kelly will work to protect our national sovereignty, military strength, and border security.

The rest of this book describes Brian Kelly's candidacy so that as had been announced in the past by those against Mr. Kelly, nobody can say that Brian Kelly is not the best candidate for America.

Chapter 3 Why is Brian Kelly Running for the US Senate

Question: Why are you running for the US Senate?
Answer: That is a very good question?

As a husband and father, my family was very important in this decision to run for office again. In 2008, I considered running and my family and I discussed it at length and I decided not to run. In 2010, I put a team together, and I saved some money and my family gave me encouragement, though they still had some trepidation about the potential impact on our family unit. We'd like to remain reasonably private and regular people. At the same time, there were other factors.

This year, eight years after I held the #1 position on the ballot for the Democratic Primary, I am running for the US Senate as a write-in candidate, because of a number of reasons. I am running as a write-in because I simply cannot afford to try to outspend the fat campaign war-chest amassed for Bob Casey. So, I am running a campaign on the cheap but with your help, I will prove that money does not trump the will of the people.

My family agrees that things are even worse for Americans this time around and Bob Casey's support for Chuck Schumer is making them worse. I would be happy to defer my candidacy to a like-minded person if one shows up. Short of that there are a lot of things that are wrong, with our country, and I would love the opportunity to get my hands dirty to help fix them. I am at the right time of my life and I see no reason why I should stand by and watch as my family's liberties, both economic and civil, are being wiped out by our own government.

Reagan had a sense of humor

You may remember Ronald Reagan's great sense of humor. Reagan, for example is credited with a number of sayings. Without me offering any commentary, you can learn a lot about why I am running for the US Senate from the fact that I really do love the following Reagan quotes.

"The nine most terrifying words in the English language are: 'I'm from the government and I'm here to help.'"

"Approximately 80 percent of our air pollution stems from hydrocarbons released by vegetation, so let's not go overboard in setting and enforcing tough emission standards from man-made sources."

"I've noticed that everyone who is for abortion has already been born."

"I am not worried about the deficit. It is big enough to take care of itself."

[Brian Kelly adds that Ronald Reagan never met Barack Obama]

"Politics is supposed to be the second-oldest profession. I have come to realize that it bears a very close resemblance to the first."

Does that help you know where I stand on those issues? There is a whole menu on this site. It is called "Platform Points." It discusses just about any point in my platform and offers where I stand on it.

In life, we are often told that we must be for something, not just against things. I am for a lot of things but one of my best ways of describing why I am running for Congress is to speak in the negative. "I do not want the government controlling my life." Yes, there is a corollary to that precept: "I do not want the government controlling your life."

I can recall some great people in my life making comments that now make so much sense. For example, Dennis Grimes Senior from Fulton Street in Wilkes-Barre, who, when told that Congress did not get much done this term, would always say: "good!" Then, of course with the twinkle in his Irish eyes, he would add a little priceless gem to make the sentence end well, and I would smile. How profound he was.

Each time Congress meets we lose more freedom. There are too many people who think that you should do this, and you should do that. It is bad news when they get into office. They want to make sure you do it and they have the power to make laws to make it mandatory. I want to let you alone to lead your own life, and I hope if you are in similar circumstance, that you will let me alone to lead my life.

I believe that freedom is our most important gift. Our forefathers shed their blood for our freedom and liberty. Freedom has no real limits but being a good person does add restrictions to freedom.

For example, I believe that in many and possibly most cases, a particular individual's freedom ends where another person's freedom begins. So, there will always be disputes between people and so it is OK to have some rules that help arbitrate man's behavior to his fellow man. My favorite rule book was created by the Founders. It is called the Constitution. Barack Obama and the 111th through 114th Congresses think they know better than the rules in this book and that is one major source of the angst in this country.

The fewer impositions of government on the people, the better. Government should get out of lives. We can handle salt, and sugar, and heat and cold. Government should worry about roads, bridges, traffic, and defense and a few other limited items.

I see no reason, for example to have a government law that outlaws beer, or two-ply toilet tissue, or red hair, or tattoos. I see no reason for laws that command that I must do something such as attend church services on Sundays -- or not attend or turn off my air conditioner in the summer (car or home) because somebody else wants me to save energy. I would not want to be commanded to use Dr. X as my family physician instead of Dr. Y. I surely would not want to have a visit scheduled with Dr. Kevorkian.

I would not want to have to use gasohol when gasoline or an alternative energy source suits my tastes. I would not want to have to buy health insurance, a pair of mittens, blue socks, a notepad, or cough medicine if I am not so inclined. I want liberty. I want freedom to make my own choices in life. On everything but abortion, I am pro-choice. On this issue I am pro Mom and pro Baby!

For me, it really is all about freedom, which is the positive of "no government control." I do not want government monitoring or controlling of my life from womb to tomb or any other area in between. I have written twenty-some additional books between my first run for Congress and now, many of which include a full copy of the Constitution of the United States.

The Constitution was created in order to form a "more perfect union," since it corrected a number of flaws in the Articles of Confederation. It is not perfect, but it is lots better than Nancy Pelosi and Harry Reid and Barack Obama making up freedom-destroying rules on the fly, as they go along.

My campaign is a very new campaign and for many it will not seem like much of a campaign. That's OK, the founding fathers would love it. If the truth be known, there is no real "campaign," just a bunch of friends who help me with great advice and my very active keyboard where I pen letters to the editor, press releases and essays for my web site. Thank you for reading this one. I hope to be able to select some "free" events in which to participate, but they are not offered frequently as incumbent politicians know that the more you know about me, the less you will like them.

The vast percentage of the people I know believe that we must fight back against a monstrous, out of control government. Those who know me believe that I would make a difference in Washington, and though they have cautioned that nobody gets elected without putting together at least a little machine, they enjoy the fact that we are doing this without any machine and with no contributions.

In 2010 my little team and I went out over three weeks and brought in 1516 signatures though I needed only 1000. Only! Try and get them. I will never do that again as I had to shut down my life and the lives of too many friends. We were out getting signatures but since all of us have some type of gainful employment, we could not have an exhaustive campaign and did not and will not try to knock on doors. It is tough enough just penning these articles.

Thank you for "listening." Don't forget to vote on November 6, 2018

Chapter 4 It's Tough Being Unknown!

"THE BIGGEST MISTAKE YOU COULD EVER MAKE IS BEING TOO AFRAID TO MAKE ONE."
~UNKNOWN

Everybody knows somebody sometime

It is not such a good thing when "everybody knows somebody sometime" and you are not on the list. When you are the new guy, sometimes the press forgets. That is my problem this year with no choice but to run as a write-in candidate to get my unique platform adopted by somebody such as Lou Barletta or by myself when elected to the Senate.

I do not think Bob Casey would be good for PA and so more than running against Casey and Barletta, I am continuing the primary and running against Bob Casey Jr. Of course, I'll take any Republican votes I can get.

I fear that if I were to bring my unique platform points as revealed in the Speech in Chapter 8 to Bob Casey's attention, he would adopt them as part of his platform and he would be unbeatable by me or by Lou Barletta. As a nobody, as much as I want these platform points adopted for the good of America, having Bob Casey Jr. back in office hurting the Trump agenda as the Senior Senator from PA would be too high a price to pay.

Many of my friends ask me how I hope to get known by people who live in any of the sixty-seven counties that make up Pennsylvania. Let me tell you, it is tough without major political financing. But, we must persevere with press releases, letters to the media, and make a speech whenever asked. To get the attention of the press, a candidate must first "press" his nose against the glass of the media outlets (Newspaper, Radio, and TV) to get their attention. I am doing that with this book and a number of press releases and letters.

Unfortunately for unknown and not-well financed candidates, in my experience in having run unsuccessfully three times, the priority of the management of media outlets is to maintain their viability by bringing in ad revenue and not giving up space or time to citizen candidates. I know that it will not be smooth sailing, but nothing ventured, nothing gained.

Fortunately, I can set up and manage web sites and I can use Facebook. Therefore, I can reach web surfers without any cost. This time, I will not have a Donate Button to accept contributions but that is OK as I won't need an accountant when it is over to figure out the financial statements. Because it is a state-wide election yard signs in the local community will not be effective, so I will save on that.

In their article, Journalism in the Digital Age, five Stanford (cs.stanford.edu) authors-- Danny Crichton, Ben Christel, Aaditya Shidham, Alex Valderrama, Jeremy Karmel, take the time to explain the absolute importance of a Fourth Estate (the media) as the most important pillar of our Democratic Republic: Too bad we have the Fake News Media instead.

Here is what they say:

"Journalism has long been regarded as an important force in government, so vital to the functioning of a democracy that it has been portrayed as an integral component of democracy itself. In 1841, Thomas Carlyle wrote, "Burke said there were Three Estates in Parliament; but, in the Reporters' Gallery yonder, there sat a Fourth

Estate more important far than they all" (On Heroes and Hero Worship).

Four years earlier, Carlyle had used the phrase in his French Revolution: "A Fourth Estate, of Able Editors, springs up, increases and multiplies; irrepressible, incalculable." Carlyle saw the press as instrumental to the birth and growth of democracy, spreading facts and opinions and sparking revolution against tyranny.

"The fact of the matter is that democracy requires informed citizens. No governing body can be expected to operate well without knowledge of the issues on which it is to rule, and rule by the people entails that the people should be informed. In a representative democracy, the role of the press is twofold: it both informs citizens and sets up a feedback loop between the government and voters.

The press makes the actions of the government known to the public, and voters who disapprove of current trends in policy can take corrective action in the next election. Without the press, the feedback loop is broken, and the government is no longer accountable to the people. The press is therefore of the utmost importance in a representative democracy. Today, the press is more concerned with making fake news than with reporting real news, so it will be a tough challenge indeed.

"Another, related, function of the press is to expose people to opinions contrary to their own. This function is perhaps the most valuable in the Internet age; while people can in theory get information about the actions of their government from online sources, it is all too easy to find opinions online that match one's own. Informed decision-making on the part of voters requires an awareness of multiple points of view, which is not likely to be obtained if voters bear the sole responsibility of seeking out information on relevant issues.

The news media provides a forum for debates to take place, as well as moderating and curating the arguments presented by all sides. It is, of course, idealistic to suppose that media give equal, or even proportional, representation to all opinions, but the fact that many media outlets present themselves as nonpartisan sources of information makes them a better forum for debate than online sources such as blogs, which are typically maintained by one individual or a small group of people with similar opinions..."

It would be nice if the mainstream media took the time to provide forums in their media to inform the public of the candidacies of all citizens running in all elections. Even if it were not every day, and the media used its power to permit short speeches to be carried on their on-line sites. The media's job in our Republic is to inform the public and let me just say they can do a far better job than what they do. When you consider that in the three times that I have run for office, the media was mostly MIA, I can say I know from experience.

I have not even been interviewed or permitted to participate in any event on Public Television, even though we the people pay for it. I was interviewed when I ran for Mayor on Election Day but the channel WBRE TV in my home town chose not to run the video. Let me repeat, the media does a disservice to the community by not informing the public of its choices.

I have never been endorsed by any media outlet as I have never been well known by their advertising departments.

Reporters and Newspaper Executives are not easy to move to your side. They do not feel obligated to assure that the public knows what each candidate has to offer.

The Press's problem in this general election season is that "Nobody expects that a guy 'who nobody knows,' will run for office." And so, I know that as a candidate, I will be very close to being summarily ignored.

I do not think that anybody in the press tries to purposely hurt me or any other candidate, but they have their favorites. From my experience in the past, even after writing letters to the editor and sending multiple press releases trying to assure the media that I am a viable candidate, I found myself excluded from much of the news coverage. Whether it was intentional or not, no media outlet tried to make up for the loss of publicity my campaigns suffered.

I would hope that regardless of how well known a candidate may be in this upcoming election, the papers and the other news media of NEPA should permit candidates to do things that help the people become informed about where they stand on the major issues of the day. In the past, I have had few vehicles provided for me that would help the people know who I am.

Thus, anybody other than an incumbent or one well-endowed by blessings (cash) can expect to be relegated to the back seat in an election.

The papers. TV, and Radio etc. should permit candidates to submit a short essay, perhaps several times during the campaign. In some media, a short essay per week might be appropriate. In others, a mere mention every now and then would be very informative for the people. The local government should also provide areas in which candidates can give speeches…but in my area, they do not.

The charter of the press is to provide news to the people, and news about who may be chosen to represent the people is worthy news indeed.

For me, the bottom line is that it is not easy for democracy to continue when the people have a tough time getting on the ballot and then they must fight against mythical forces to convince even their neighbors that they are serious in the endeavor. My political friends say that is the nature of the beast. I say, the beast is the problem.

Thank you for reading and / or visiting my site:

Chapter 5 Brian Kelly Is a JFK Democrat

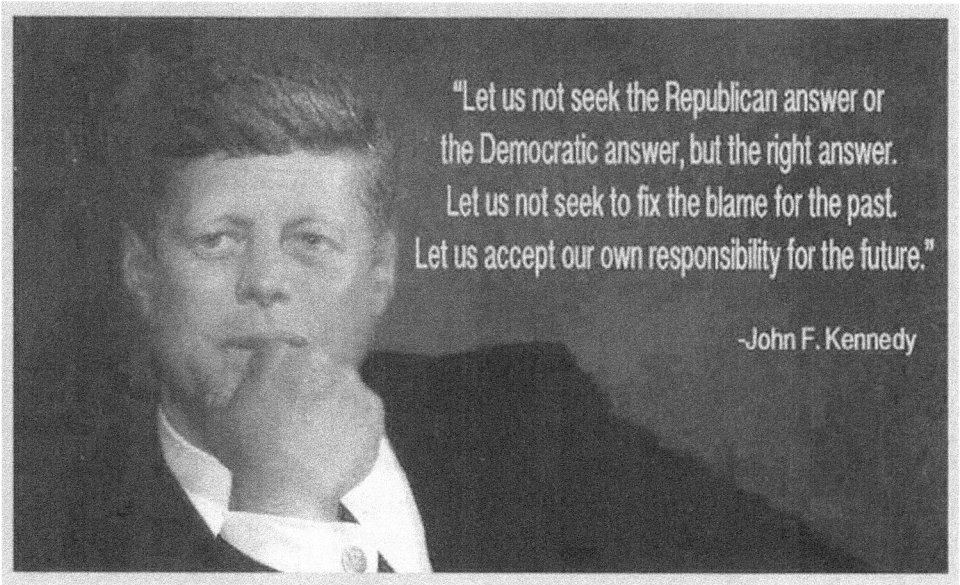

"Let us not seek the Republican answer or the Democratic answer, but the right answer. Let us not seek to fix the blame for the past. Let us accept our own responsibility for the future."

-John F. Kennedy

Being A JFK Democrat

You may wonder why I am a JFK Democrat instead of a conservative Republican? The fact is that neither party is perfect for me. I am for business but not for unbridled corporate power. I am for unions but not for thug tactics in the workplace and I am not for forced unionism.

I worked for IBM for 23 years and at the time, IBM never had nor needed a union. Corporations should treat employees right and unions should be for the employees and not on the same team as the managers. At IBM, the founders believed that if you take care of the people, the people will take care of the business. It worked!

I am pro-life, and I am against selling baby parts and live brains, though some legislators such as say, Bob Casey Jr., the incumbent, forget this. Deep down most Americans are pro-life. Who wants to kill babies when they are the most vulnerable--when they have not made their first goo or gaw?

I do not believe in protecting smelts and trees if it causes harm to human beings. God made human beings with dominion over all life, and though we must be just caretakers of this awesome responsibility, it should not mean that humans must starve or be cold or freeze in the wintertime to please somebody's twisted agenda.

In many ways some of the great ambitions of the Democratic Party leaders to create an equal world where there is no injustice has placed human beings per se in the back seat and has elevated non-humans to a status not intended by God. What good is it to freeze in the winter simply because the EPA has chosen to ban coal? I grew up with a coal stove in my living room and kitchen as did my wife, and we are still healthy. Plus, we (the USA) have plenty of coal for the rest of the world. Why shut off the spigot? Why? It makes no sense. China is killing us economically using coal!

Don't you think that protecting unborn babies is more important than protecting turtle eggs? Since it is a crime to destroy turtle eggs, at a minimum, it should also be a crime to kill an unborn child? Who is not pro baby? I think the big shot elite leaders of the Democratic Party have begun to endorse philosophies that give Government, rather than God, supreme power. I believe that God rules supreme above all else. When was the last time you were at a deathbed and heard the grieving family praying to the government?

Though recently I have come to like the philosophies of populists and conservatives like Marco Rubio and Donald Trump and Ben Carson and Ted Cruz. I am not for communists such as Bernie Sanders nor for wannabe communists such as Hillary Clinton. There is no good choice on the Democrat side. Sorry! JFK is sorely needed!

Like the Republican nominees, I do not think that corporations were meant to dominate individuals. I also think that American corporations have an obligation in exchange for the privilege of operating in America to care for their employees and to help do everything in their power to protect and create American Jobs.

Hiring illegal aliens must be verboten!

Republicans and many rich Democrats even prominent Democrats such as John Kerry and the Heinz Company have no problem taking jobs overseas. Additionally, they have no problem trying to reduce the American wage to as low as possible by bringing in illegal foreign workers to force the wages down.

Neither party wants to enforce our immigration laws. Republicans want lower wages and Democrats see a huge voter pool in those who are granted amnesty. I am for safe and secure borders and I believe in an America for Americans. If foreigners can live legally within our borders according to our laws, I am for that also. But, American citizens, that's us folks, must come first instead of last.

I would like to share with you, information on a site that describes how to be a conservative (JFK) Democrat. My philosophies for the most part fit this description.
http://www.ehow.com/how_2090667_be-conservative-democrat.html

How to Be a Conservative Democrat
Contributor: By eHow Contributing Writer
Article Rating: (11 Ratings)

In politics sometimes, it seems easy to categorize a person by their party affiliation. A Republican is conservative, and a Democrat is liberal. That is too limiting and shortsighted. Party affiliation does not eliminate individual thought. Defying these stereotypes is not always easy but is what democracy is based on--freedom of thought and choice.

Instructions for being a conservative Democrat

1. Step 1
Believe in small government. Small government means limiting the sprawling bureaucracy that invades people's lives and tries to tell them how to live those lives. Small government also means limiting monetary waste in government that comes with oversized government programs.

2. Step 2
Understand that there are services that the government needs to offer. While the conservative Democrat is against big government, they realize that some social programs are necessary for the country to thrive.

3. Step 3
Realize that a strong military force is a good. While curtailing government spending is prudent, it should not be at the expense of the nation's military. Even in times of peace, a strong military can be a deterrent to other aggressive countries and governments.

4. Step 4
Sympathize with the working class. A conservative democrat understands that the working class is the backbone that built this country. Conservative Democrats keep this in mind whenever taking issue with a policy or ideology.

5. Step 5
Focus on education and family values. Education and family values are an important part of the core values of the conservative Democrat. Education is what made this country a world leader and needs to be the focus of a conservative Democrats political agenda.

6. Step 6
Consider free market capitalism a positive endeavor. A conservative Democrat understands that the free market and capitalism empower the individual to make her own destiny.

For Democrats who feel as I do about life, I am clearly your candidate for Pennsylvania, and I would appreciate your vote.

Chapter 6 Mr. Smith Goes to Washington

Jimmy Stewart from the movie, Mr. Smith Goes to Washington is a guiding light for my campaign. The people like Jimmy Stewart and the honest guys like Jefferson Smith are indispensable for a great democracy / republic.

Mr. Smith Goes to Washington

Ladies and Gentlemen, I would like to present myself. My name is Jefferson Smith and I am going to Washington—if you select me of course.

Jimmy Stewart is one of my favorite actors of all time. He is as Americana as it gets with the perfect touch of honesty that makes even men admire the actor and the character the actor is playing. My favorite movie of all time is "It's A Wonderful Life." It gets me every time. Remember the big pot of cash the neighbors brought in to George Bailey, so he could keep the Building and Loan going. Well, that's how I think America should be. Every hard-working American deserves a break.

What George Bailey did not need was the government stealing from his neighbors so that he could go to college and to heck with Pottersville. Well, it would have been Pottersville if George had not stayed to help all the people in Bedford Falls with his dad's Building and Loan Company. Government intervention creates Pottersvilles and good neighbors create the likes of Bedford Falls. Let's let good people be good people again rather than taking so much from them that Mr. Potter is the only one left with any money.

Mr. Smith Goes to Washington exudes the same emotion from the viewer. It was another of Frank Capra's big hits and Jimmy Stewart as Jefferson Smith is as down to earth as George Bailey. I don't propose that I can do as good a job for Northeastern PA as Jefferson Smith did for his constituency. However, I am as much a babe in the woods as far as politics go as Mr. Smith.

I am running for office to help fight the same type of corruption that Smith faced when he went to Washington. I am up to the task and I am ready to fight to make America, America again. There is nothing separating me from my chance other than this general election and your write-in. I thank you very much in advance for the vote.

You may know that Kelly is the second most common family name in Ireland (after Murphy). It is the 69th most popular surname in the United States. Kelly in many ways is like Jones and Smith.

And so, will you indulge me please as I say again. My name is Mr. Smith, and I am going to Washington. I can't get there without your help.

Think of the corrupt conditions that existed in this famous movie as Mr. Smith, played by Jimmy Stewart. Smith was little more than a bumpkin, when he first went into the Washington swamp of iniquity. For Smith, it was the US Senate. He was the naive and idealistic Jefferson Smith, the leader of the Boy Rangers. In Washington, Smith soon discovers many of the shortcomings of the political process as his earnest goal of a national boys' camp leads to a conflict with the state's corrupt political boss, Jim Taylor.

Taylor first tries to corrupt Smith and then later attempts to destroy Smith through a made-up scandal. Smith conducts a filibuster and finally sways everybody to not pass the healthcare bill. Wouldn't that be nice! (It was the Boy Rangers Bill). Smith would be working to get the bill repealed if it were passed, and the movie would have taken a bit longer. Kelly will make the repeal of the 2700 page bill a priority and will replace it with an EMTALA-like bill in the neighborhood of 4 to 8 pages. Additionally, Brian has a great plan for illegal interlopers and he will wipe out all student debt now and Boost Social Security so that the elderly can keep living in their homesteads.

Stranger things have happened. I hope to be like your Mr. Smith if you select me. And, so, I ask you to send me to Washington to serve in the United States Senate instead of Bob Casey. I hope there are approximately 32 additional like-thinking Senators sworn in when I have the honor to take office in January 2019. I want to thank you all. Thank you very much.

Chapter 7 Rush Limbaugh On the Issues

Rush is very opinionated

Before I go over the Brian Kelly Platform points in the last chapter, through the speech that I originally wrote for Congressman Lou Barletta, permit me to examine the issues and Rush's opinion on the issues.

The facts in this section are according to http://www.ontheissues.org/Rush_Limbaugh.htm.

We'll go from issues A through Z and show the bullets describing Rush's position on each of the issues examined. Some are taken from the show and demonstrate his keen sense of humor.

On Abortion

- ✓ Don't require colleges to pay for students' contraception. (Sep 2012)
- ✓ Feminists are pro-choice as an avenue of power over men. (Mar 2011)
- ✓ 2008: A pro-choice GOP VP would destroy the Party. (Jan 2010)
- ✓ Roe v. Wade is bad law; let states decide. (Jul 1992)
- ✓ Women obsessed with abortion & intolerance are "feminazis". (Jul 1992)

On Budget & Economy

- ✓ QE3 equals printing money equals inflation. (Sep 2012)
- ✓ At Obama's inauguration: "I hope he fails". (Mar 2011)
- ✓ TARP is not constitutional, and unsustainable. (Feb 2009)

On Civil Rights

- ✓ Call NBA teams "gangs"; fans go to watch Crips vs. Bloods. (Mar 2011)
- ✓ Feminism gives unattractive women access to mainstream. (Mar 2011)
- ✓ 1995: AIDS is the only federally-protected virus. (Mar 2011)
- ✓ Marriage is between one man and one woman. (Aug 2010)
- ✓ We need the Walmart voter & the NASCAR voter. (Feb 2009)
- ✓ Abolish P.C. speech codes at colleges. (Jul 1993)
- ✓ N.O.W. supports liberal feminists, not women in general. (Jul 1992)
- ✓ Chivalry is male chauvinism to radical feminists. (Jul 1992)
- ✓ Men ogling women is part of gender equality. (Jul 1992)

On Corporations

- ✓ Calling the rich lucky is like Mao's Cultural Revolution. (Apr 2014)
- ✓ Capitalists give you jobs; don't assault them. (Feb 2009)

On Crime

- ✓ Only thing cruel about death penalty is last-minute stays. (Jul 1992)

On Drugs

- ✓ Anti-smoking campaigners will celebrate legal marijuana. (Dec 2012)
- ✓ Laws against selling drugs and using drugs are good laws. (Mar 2011)
- ✓ Rush Limbaugh on Education
- ✓ Discourages education; schools screw up children. (Mar 2011)
- ✓ Multiculturalism is historical revisionism. (Jul 1993)

✓ Don't encourage homosexuality by teaching it in grade school. (Jul 1993)

On Education (School Choice)

✓ Parents are tired of sending kids to inferior schools. (Jan 2001)
✓ Vigorously promote educational choice and vouchers. (Jul 1993)

On Energy & Oil

✓ 2007: Phasing out incandescent light bulbs is nanny state. (Apr 2012)
✓ Cap-and-trade is a conspiracy to benefit Wall Street. (Mar 2011)
✓ OpEd: Country's leading denier of global climate change. (Mar 2011)
✓ Global warming is a religion; only God can destroy earth. (Mar 2011)
✓ Global warming is bogus. (Jan 2001)

On Environment

✓ Let's count all the disproven environmental myths. (Jul 1993)
✓ Animals have no fundamental rights; only people do. (Jul 1992)
✓ Animal rights movement is secular humanism vs. Bible. (Jul 1992)
✓ Economic growth is key to environmental cleanup. (Jul 1992)
✓ Gaia worship is religion of secular environmentalists. (Jul 1992)
✓ Priority on people, not on spotted owls. (Jul 1992)
✓

On Families & Children

✓ Feminazis say all sex is rape, even the sex in marriage. (Mar 2011)

On Foreign Policy

✓ Gorbachev's ouster gives world peace a chance; end Gorbasms. (Jul 1992)

On Free Trade

✓ Support for NAFTA cited in 1993 Gore-Perot debate. (Sep 2011)
✓ NAFTA lets unskilled Mexicans do our unskilled labor. (Mar 2011)

On Government Reform

✓ Citizens United gives corporations same rights as unions. (Jul 2012)
✓ House banking scandal involved crimes with taxpayer funds. (Jul 1992)
✓ Congress should not exempt itself from laws. (Jul 1992)

On Gun Control

✓ Handguns enhance safety & reduce crime rates. (Dec 2012)
✓ Rush Limbaugh on Health Care
✓ 1994: Whitewater is about health care. (Nov 2003)
✓ Health care has problems, but no crisis for drastic change. (Jul 1993)
✓ Deregulate health care; government is the problem. (Jul 1993)

✓ Drug abuse & unsafe sex cause AIDS, not homophobia. (Jul 1992)

On Homeland Security

✓ Fiscal cliff cuts defense without any political price. (Nov 2012)
✓ Defense Authorization Act is total authoritarianism. (Jan 2012)
✓ Al Qaeda people would surrender to get treatment like Gitmo. (Oct 2008)
✓ Nobody got physically injured in Abu Ghraib scandal. (Oct 2005)
✓ No women in combat. (Jul 1993)
✓ No gays in army; not a place for social experiments. (Jul 1993)
✓ Do not subject women to the horrors of combat. (Jul 1992)

On Immigration

✓ Legal immigrants should join together in common culture. (Feb 2017)
✓ 2005: Mexican illegal immigrants are an invasive species. (Mar 2011)
✓ Enforce the law, secure the borders, and legalize some. (May 2010)

On Jobs

✓ 1980s tax cuts created jobs by "trickle down". (Jul 1993)

On Principles & Values

✓ 80% of listeners identify themselves as conservatives. (Jan 2012)
✓ Operation Chaos: Republicans vote for Hillary in primary. (Mar 2011)

- ✓ Criticizes Democrats for not following the Constitution. (Jan 2011)
- ✓ I want Obama to fail, because I want America to survive. (Feb 2009)
- ✓ Demonstrates the absurdity of official media dogma. (Dec 2003)
- ✓ 1994 Freshman GOP called themselves "The Ditto-Head Caucus". (Jun 1995)
- ✓ "New Democrat" really means old liberal social engineer. (Jul 1993)
- ✓ Constitution only works in a moral society. (Jul 1993)
- ✓ Liberalism poisons the soul and destroys character. (Jul 1993)
- ✓ Establishment clause does not preclude school prayer. (Jul 1992)

On Social Security

- ✓ No issue stance yet recorded by OnTheIssues.org.
- ✓ Check the Brian Kelly for US Senate platform in the speech in Chapter 8 for a few more good points

On Tax Reform

- ✓ JFK believed in tax cuts to stimulate economy. (Oct 2012)
- ✓ No trigger on tax cuts, "trigger lock" instead. (Feb 2001)
- ✓ Targeted tax cuts make middle-class beholden to liberals. (Feb 2001)
- ✓ Tax fairness is simple: Give our money back. (Feb 2001)

On Technology

- ✓ Never fired from any radio show due to conservatism. (Mar 2011)
- ✓ First to combine entertainment and political opinion. (Mar 2011)

✓ Responsible for idea that Obama requires a teleprompter. (Mar 2011)
✓ "Drive-by media" means the state controls what is broadcast. (Mar 2011)
✓ Founded radio show immediately after "Fairness Doctrine". (Nov 2009)
✓ Broadcast's "Fairness Doctrine" breaches First Amendment. (Jul 1993)
✓ Talk Radio threatens liberals because they can't control it. (Jul 1992)

On War & Peace

✓ Claimed WMDs in Iraq even after Bush admitted no WMDs. (Mar 2011)
✓ Democrats want war in Iraq to fail. (Feb 2009)

Welfare & Poverty

✓ War on poverty has failed; welfare destroys human potential. (Feb 2009)
✓ The poor get all the benefits in this country. (Jun 1997)

Chapter 8 Rush Would Love Brian Kelly's US Senate Platform

Note from your author and Senate Candidate Brian W. Kelly

Brian Kelly when Chief Technology Officer College Misericordia circa 1994

No, I don't look like this anymore, but I did look like this when as the chief technology officer at College Misericordia in the 1990's, I began to pay a lot more attention to what goes on in our government. The College paid for this picture.

By now, I admit that I am not too happy with what I discovered about government and politics in our country. That, and because like you, I could not afford a full-bore Senatorial campaign, is why I am running as a write-in candidate for the US Senate.

Ask yourself this question: Would you hire any Congressman in America today to run your business—even to babysit your kids? Me neither! Yet, we hire them through the electoral process to run the most complex country that ever was—the United States of America. It is clear that at some point we must begin to make better choices. Why not start in 2018?

I think the best way to begin this book is to give you the campaign speech that I had written to give the first time I would find a forum in a cost-free venue. There is a lot in this speech but then again, there are many issues today in America. As I review the contents of this speech below, I wish that I could make the speech shorter and at the same time more comprehensive, so you fully know what the platform is all about and why it is worthy of your consideration. I have done my best, but I do admit that this is not one of my shortest speeches. Thank you.

Originally, I wrote this speech for Congressman Lou Barletta, hoping he would adopt the platform elements in this speech as his own. I believe the Congressman likes these ideas but as he is running for Senator as a Republican, it would be difficult to convince officials in the Republican Party of their worth. It would be tough to push a platform that may have a negative effect on the budget cuts Republicans are seeking. And, so, I decided to go it alone, and instead of expecting the man who I believe may still become Senator Barletta present these ideas for America, I will do the job myself under my own write-in candidacy.

Just write me in.

B-R-I-A-N K-E-L-L-Y

Don't type the dashes.

Campaign Update August 3, 2018

This is the day after the Donald Trump Rally in Wilkes-Barre, my home town, on behalf of Republican Lou Barletta for the US Senate. As a result of that 1 hour and sixteen-minute rally, Donald Trump's phenomenal speech, his endorsement of Lou Barletta, and an equally great and inspiring speech by Senate Candidate Lou Barletta, I have decided to endorse Congressman Lou Barletta for the US Senate. I am as much **opposed** to Senator Robert 'Sleepin Bob' Casey as I am **in favor** of a great American, Lou Barletta, a man who shares most of my values.

For those Democrats who historically will not vote for a Republican under any circumstances, or those Democrats desiring the package of unique pro-American legislation that I have developed in the past, I encourage you to make a better choice for the US Senate than Bob Casey. Pennsylvania needs a great US Senator. Casey has not been that man and his concern for the people is getting worse, not better. Lou Barletta is the best choice. However, if you must vote Democrat, remember that Bob Casey is not for the people of Pennsylvania. Rather than vote for Casey, you may feel free to write my name in for United States Senator B-R-I-A-N K-E-L-L-Y. I am a registered Democrat. Thank you.

At the PA Wilkes-Barre Rally, President Trump and Congressman Barletta netted out the same negative case against Bob Casey, Jr as a legislator. Trump began by saying the younger Casey was boring, a nobody in Washington who does what Democratic leaders tell him. I don't think I ever met him, Trump said. Bob Casey is for open borders, Trump asserted, again raising the specter of violent immigrants from Central America overrunning the country.

Barletta and Trump noted that Casey is a pro-abortion, anti-second amendment socialist by his record and he expects Casey to be calling for the abolition of the Immigration and Customs Enforcement (ICE) agency, a favorite cause on the left. He more or less said that Chuck Schumer says "Jump," and Bob Casey says: "How high?" Then, every, time, he goes ahead and jumps. Though Casey says he is not anti-ICE, he also says he is anti-abortion and then votes pro-abortion in almost all cases, such as his opposition to Judges Gorsich and Cavanaugh. For twelve years, Bob Casey Jr. has been the epitome of a do-nothing politician, choosing not to do the people's business. It is time for Casey to make a graceful exit.

Like me, Lou Barletta is for the entire Trump agenda, especially the Wall, and that will be good for America. The only thing that we disagree on is a detailed solution that I put together in several books this year that squarely address resident illegal foreign nationals, Fair COLAs for Seniors, and a major economic stimulus by solving the student loan crisis.

End of Campaign Update

I never received a reply from Rush when I sent this speech to him about my Senate platform. I knew he would love it. This speech, which I had written when I planned a formal announcement of my write-in candidacy for the office of US Senator from Pennsylvania. It offers great solutions for Obamacare, Immigration, Seniors and Social Security, and Millennials and Student Loans. I bet as soon as Rush reads this again, I will get a call to be on the show.

With this speech, I will be able to show off a platform that can make seniors and millennials whole, fix the problem with illegal foreign nationals in the shadows, remove the need for sanctuary cities, and the problems with DACA, and help Americans afford health care insurance again.

Rush, I know you will love this platform because it solves a ton of problems and puts bucks in some folk's pockets who have forgotten how nice a dollar looks.

God bless all of you who have purchased and read this book. Now you can enjoy the speech announcing Brian Kelly's candidacy for the US Senate against two-term Democratic incumbent Robert P. Casey Jr. It is so right on for today that I enjoy it every time I read or edit it.

As you will see in the beginning of the speech, I designed it for an audience full of people. I have already had some reaction to my running from people in my inner circle.

Here it is:

Fellow Citizens,

Language is inadequate to express my gratitude for the privilege of submitting before you my candidacy to represent the fine people of Pennsylvania as your US Senator.

I would also like to thank you for the fine welcome, which you all have extended to me on this occasion. As I look out in my mind's eye, I see a vast sea of human faces who share a common interest, as do I, about the greatest questions of our times. Beyond occasionally agitating the mind, they now dominate the concerns of all Pennsylvanians and U.S. citizens, underlying the foundations of our free institutions. Let us all make sure that freedom never becomes just another word for nothing left to lose.

The reaction of my U.S. Senate candidacy by the people of Pennsylvania has been quite heartening. We have a president whose interest quite simply is to "Make America Great Again." By contrast, the embedded establishment and liberal leftovers in the SWAMP, have no interest in performing what is good for our country. They are doing their best to undermine our president, without any repercussions, aided and abetted by a corrupt media, instead of building bridges to work for the good of all Americans.

It is no longer acceptable for a Democrat or a Republican to be a Never-Trumper. Donald Trump is our president and his platform is my platform and when elected, I hope the extras in my platform that I introduce in this speech, become part of the Trump platform.

We all know that "Never-Trumpers" will never hold office again. Democrats such as Bob Casey Jr., my opponent, simply adore the establishment's impediments to the president's agenda with a media whose interests are as adverse to the American people as the British press was during Colonial Times.

The Democrats and the Republican Never-Trumpers in the Senate, House, and the federal bureaucracy and the degenerate mainstream press have done everything they can to thwart the will of 62,979,636 people who voted to clean out the SWAMP with a fresh new presidential administration.

The legendarily venal Hillary Clinton lost the election after the public saw through her charade; yet she continues to parade around the world blaming everything from her own adoring fans at The New York Times, to white women like her, to the DNC, and probably even the cows in Wisconsin, a state she famously lost after taking it so for granted, she never visited.

She even blames the FBI and it never occurs to anyone that the best way to avoid an untimely FBI intervention in a political campaign is to *not run for President while under federal criminal investigation*. And all the while, Senator Casey stood by submissively, applauding and enabling this farce of a candidacy. It is time for the country to move on. She lost, now get over it. We've had twelve years of Casey and that's about as much as any man or woman in America can stand.

I am running for the US Senate to reclaim this seat which rightfully belongs to its people, not the extrinsic interests controlling our politicians who would tear the Constitution in half without hesitation if it would please their donors and cheerleaders in the mainstream media. Despite the shameless lack of virtue that defines the top echelons of our government, our country itself is replete with honest citizens who would be humbled to work on behalf of their fellow countrymen and women. That is why I am running for the US Senate against one of the biggest icons of mainstream mediocrity and corruption, Mr. Bob Casey Jr.

Casey Jr. caters only to the whining anti-Trump crowd who wants to turn every trivial post on Facebook into a new Cuban Missile Crisis. Despite the voters in even his home state rejecting the rank duplicity of former Secretary Clinton and her bleak vision of hopelessness and sovereign state decline, Senator Casey never lifted a finger to help the people who support our president, despite the fact that we outnumber the opposition right here in Pennsylvania. But to him-- that's Bob Casey, folks; we do not even exist.

The Bob Casey Jr. that we all see is a do-nothing Senator who would prefer to turn the US into a globalist abyss rather than support its sovereignty or its people's dignity. Meanwhile, our great president is trying to find everybody a high-paying job by making it easier to conduct business in our country. I intend to help President Trump protect us from such parasitic interests.

If there is one principle most cherished in all free governments, it is that which asserts the exclusive right of a free people to form and adopt their own fundamental laws, to manage and regulate their own internal affairs and domestic institutions. That is under constant attack by Mr. Casey and his legions of Clinton dead-enders.

Electing representatives of the people is not a triviality, but rather the expression of the most fundamental right of self-government. Without it, of course, this great United States would be like any other country in the world. It would not be the exceptional republic, which we the people have enjoyed since our own Declaration of Independence.

To say that I am honored to be here today presenting my candidacy for the US Senate, would be the understatement of the ages. Thank you for your reception and hospitality. I assure you that if elected, I will provide Pennsylvania and the United States of America the best representation in the US Senate of which I am capable. You can be sure of that.

We have many issues today of which the people are concerned. My plan in this address is to limit discussion to just four of the most prominent. My candidacy uniquely addresses each of the four as no other candidate for any US office has ever been able to do. I hope you will find the elements of my platform a welcome refreshment and inclusive of precepts that we all embrace and recognize as sincere and necessary.

My format will be to be present each issue by area of concern and then offer the specific solution which is part of my unique platform. The issues and solutions will be presented one by one in the following four topical areas:

#1—Obamacare.

#2—Illegal Immigration.

#3—Student Debt Crisis Wipe Out All Student Debt Now!

#4—Social Security's Cost-of-Living Fraud – Boost Social Security Now!

My pledge is to put forth legislation when elected to help address all four issues as well as full support for the platform points in Chapter 7 and the Trump agenda. Let's discuss the unique four-points above, one by one, starting with Obamacare.

Obamacare

The first problem on the list is #1 because over 54% of Americans say that the availability and affordability of healthcare is their #1 issue. Despite Obama's empty promises, many of us cannot keep our favorite doctors nor can we retain an affordable health plan that meets our needs. The costs have been so prohibitive that many Americans have forestalled doctor's visits with often grave consequences. We all know that despite what Bob Casey would offer you, Obamacare is a disaster.

My solution to Obamacare begins with clarity and definitive purpose. We start with a one-line repeal. The beast is vanquished. Following the repeal, we envision a plethora of competing less expensive alternatives provided by the marketplace without current tyrannical government controls.

Illegal Immigration

In February 2004, Arizona Senator John McCain recognized via Border Patrol reports that nearly four million people crossed our borders "illegally" each year following the Reagan amnesty in 1986. Nonetheless, the fraudulent press insists that the total count of illegal immigrants residing in the United States is eleven million, a mathematical impossibility if Border Patrol figures are to be believed. And of these millions of foreigners, countless amounts receive welfare while, contrary to popular mythology, very few actually work in agriculture.

There may be as many as 60 million and perhaps more illegal foreign nationals living in the United States today. While some individuals in this group may contribute to our society, on balance this is outweighed by the group's overall negative effect on our resources, whether they be drained by government assistance, lost employment opportunities for American citizens, or criminal offenses. It is amazing how effective the fake-ID business is in turning illegal aliens into fake citizens who are thus enabled to enjoy American rights and privileges.

According to the 2011 GAO report entitled "Criminal Alien Statistics," the cost of crimes by illegal foreign nationals is $8.1 billion per year, and that's without even considering the incomprehensibly larger emotional toll this takes on families whose priceless loved ones can never be replaced.

If elected, I will introduce two pieces of legislation that will solve this problem of illegal residents in the shadows once and for all. Besides many other benefits, it stands to save the U.S. over $1 Trillion per year in addition to major reductions in crime. The two solutions are known as pay-to-go and the resident visa program.

Pay-to-Go

It costs taxpayers $30,000 per year on the average, per illegal alien in America. Each illegal resident and their dependent children, who signs up for Pay to Go, on the way back to the home country, will receive a one-time $20,000 stipend plus the individual expense back to the home country. With a cost of $30,000 per year to support unwelcome interlopers, the taxpayer savings begins year one and continues at $30,000 per year forever. Not a bad deal for Americans.

The program therefore quietly accommodates family reunification in the home country. A family of five for example, could do quite well back home after receiving $100,000 in stipends from Uncle Sam. Reuniting families in their own countries is a good idea for them and for America. The savings in welfare means there is no cost in year one and in year 2, the savings equal $30,000 for each person who "goes." back home, never to return.

Resident Visa

Those who do not want to leave the US can sign up, be vetted, and eventually be approved for the Resident Visa. The visa will cost $200.00 to cover vetting in year one and it will be renewable every year thereafter for $100.00 To get a Resident Visa, a former interloper would agree to all stipulations after registering. Stipulations would include full initial vetting; onsite renewal vetting; keep existing jobs; new jobs for Americans first; no voting; no citizenship; no welfare and no freebies of any kind. Everybody is not automatically approved. After vetting, those not approved for the resident visa program may use the Pay-to-Go program to aid in their relocation.

As the program would entail 100% participation from illegal residents, estimates are as high as $500 billion per year cost savings in total for those who choose to go or for those who choose to stay using the no-welfare resident visa. Another $500 billion will be reclaimed over time for lost wages. Additionally, if we can figure a way for countries to reclaim their criminals, there is another $8.1 billion to be recovered.

Once the program is in effect, there would be no more illegal aliens in the country. Resident Visa holders would be legal and so there would be no shadows. There would be no need for DACA and no need for Sanctuary cities Let me repeat that. All issues with DACA would be over and Sanctuary Cities would be a thing of the past because there would be no shadows and no illegal interlopers.

Two additional programs are the part of my platform that I would now like to introduce. Like the resident alien plans, no other candidate for public office includes these great programs in their platform. You are going to love these.

These two new programs offer the promise of a positive effect on the health of the economy and both will contribute to improving it for American citizens of all ages to live well in this country. The first is about wiping out all student debt and the second is about offering Social Security recipients increased benefits to make up for fraudulent cost of living increases based on an intentionally fraudulent consumer price index.

Student Debt is Huge

If we look at the $1.48 Trillion dollars in student loan debt that more and more young adults simply cannot repay, some have asked: "Why do our young people no longer matter?" Do they matter?

We live in an age when everybody seems to have a reason to pick on millennials. They would not loan a "spoiled" millennial "ingrate" as much as a dollar for a cup of coffee.

Whether millennials are deserving of the bad rap or not, they represent a lost generation of our society. For the sake of all of America, they need to be invited back in. We all have student loan debtors in our families – sons, daughters, nephews, nieces, even grandparents and parents when we consider cosigners.

I plan to offer legislation when first elected to make sure we solve this nasty American problem. There have been many other debt reliefs in our history but none that could deliver such an immediate benefit to so many actual Americans all at once. The upside would be overwhelming, a joint humanitarian return and a major economic return far greater than any bailout in history. Let's consider.

A Bailout is a Bailout?

Many of us remember bailouts of the past from 2007 onward. We had bank bailouts, auto company bailouts, TARP bailouts and many other unnamed bailouts. Did any of these help your family? Of course not. Bailout fever began right before Obama became President and continued. The President managed all of the money—trillions. He chose not to give a dime to help student loan debt but spared no expense showering the degenerate financial institutions that owned his candidacy with gold.

Mike Collins, a Forbes Magazine contributor whose expertise focuses on manufacturing and government policy (not the former beloved magistrate of Wilkes-Barre who shares the same name) had this to say:

"Most people think that the big bank bailout was the $700 billion that the treasury department used to save the banks during the financial crash in September of 2008. But this is a long way from the truth because the bailout [ten years later] is still ongoing.

The Special Inspector General for TARP's summary of the bailout says that the total commitment of government is $16.8 trillion dollars with the $4.6 trillion already paid out. The [same] banks are now larger and still too big to fail. But it isn't just the government bailout money that tells the story of the bailout. This is a story about lies, cheating, and a multi-faceted corruption, which was often criminal."

Like most elements of his presidency, Obama made the situation worse when he commandeered the student loans from Sallie Mae and other lenders. The government now pulls in more than $50 billion a year from charging high interest rates to student borrowers. The Obama Student Loan Company charged 6.8% as a student interest rates. The CBO estimates that the interest rate on these loans could quickly be reduced from 6.8 percent to 5.3 percent if Obama had not earmarked the profit from the backs of students to subsidize Obamacare.

Not only were millennials duped into huge college loans when they were so young that Clearasil was one of their major expenses, they were duped into believing Obama was in their corner.

I believe these student victims deserve a break. They are now adults. Some stuck with huge cosign tabs are grandparents on Social security. The government actually garnishes their SSR to pay back the Obama loans.

The federal government is putting up $16.8 trillion dollars as of 2018 to big banks, and other nameless faces receiving bailouts. We still do not know who is getting our money. Yet students who are still being victimized by usury were preyed on as 17-year- olds by admissions counsellors for an all-but worthless college education leading to no job. If given the choice would you be helping the big banks or our own kids?

What do the people think about Student Debt?

Four in ten Americans believe that President Trump's administration should forgive all federal student debt in order to help stimulate the economy, according to a reasonably new survey revealed in 2017. As time goes by as more Americans realize we are excluding a full generation of Americans in our economy, this number will increase from a simple majority to an overwhelming endorsement of wiping out this scurrilous unfair debt as soon as possible. We should bring these 48 million students back into the American way of life as soon as possible.

The largest share blame for the student debt crisis lies with the promises made by over-zealous admissions counsellors convincing kids to sign up for $100,000 loans. No American can want a full generation of other Americans to be left behind in the Trump economy. We need this debt eradicated now and to install safeguards so that seventeen-year-olds in the future are never asked again to sign up for a life in debtor's prison.

According to MoneyTips.com, attitudes have changed from a time when Americans thought college students should be punished for making bad choices to today, when we could use 48 million new spenders in our economy. They would be unleashed into a world of productivity if no longer burdened with massive debt. Many of us know first-hand the consequences of this debt burden. Though millennials may not be the most gracious in asking for help, they are Americans, not DACA immigrants, and they need our help now.

The raw economic fact regardless of your philosophical preference is that spenders with the greatest potential to spend today are not spending at all in real numbers because of student debt. They are not getting married. They are not having families and they are not buying homes. We must solve this scourge on our country so that this generation can produce other generations of Americans.

Our children are not MS-13 members in disguise; there are our kids. American kids. They were snookered to join academia for what they were deceived into believing was an indispensable college degree by depraved loan sharks. Let's give them a full chance. It costs a university nothing when their students with huge loans fail. Please let that sink in.

Let me review the plight of young American college attendees and graduates. Barely out of adolescence, these young Americans were wheedled into commitments based on fraudulent promises by admissions counselors and financial institutions. It was unfair to pit experienced loan sharks against adolescent teenagers. The students were further damned by a paid-for Congress, whose lobbyists insisted that these select few with student debt, distinct from all of the others in America, had no opportunity for any relief in the bankruptcy courts.

Non-college graduates with a trillion dollars in credit card debt are still able to obtain full relief from the courts. Why did Congress exclude these former teenagers, who clearly have been the biggest victims of loan-sharking organized racketeering ever seen in America? Why?

I am pledging today to solve this problem as soon as I can. I am ready to take action. I hope you all agree. Let's help these young Americans before they are lost forever.

Young teenagers were told all through high school that the best ticket for a successful life is a college education. Is this true today? Their salaries often lag behind even those of non-college educated professionals such as plumbers, electricians, computer repair personnel, operating engineers, and more. Because of their reliance on these deliberately false misrepresentations, they now owe an approximate average of $50,000 in student debt while their admissions counsellors and loan sharks revel in riches, in their Mercedes, BMW's, and third vacation home on the lake.

Unscrupulous malefactors with self-interested agendas persuaded America's teenagers, many so young they still had Acne vulgaris, to dig themselves huge financial holes with no escape. Universities are at least partly responsible for their unfulfilled promises. Don't you think? We must also consider what liability they may share in compensating this lost generation where one out of six student borrowers must default today, a figure that only increases with time.

Removing this debt may not fully compensate for the bad hand they were dealt, but its consequent increase in economic activity will benefit all of us. It will boost the US economy beyond expectations. We are already giving bailouts of $17 billion to obscenely rich people in corporate shadows. Right now, we need a mere 10% of that to pay for the write-off of student debt without hurting taxpayers and without putting any banks under. The savings over three years, for example from the resident visa program alone pays off all the student debt that exists today. Why support illegal aliens when we can help Americans?

One last point. It helps to recall that President Obama increased the National Debt by $9.1 Trillion in just eight years, hoping to assure that illegal aliens had all the resources they needed to take as many American jobs as they could. This is six times the amount of debt owed by young Americans. Obama nearly doubled our debt. And what do we have to show for that? As is typical for the Obama years, the answer is frankly... nothing. By contrast, debt relief for our young Americans will be *visibly* positive in its impact.

So, let's say Congress wipes out all student debt because it is the fair thing to do. How do we prevent this from every happening again? For this, I thank my great friend, Dennis Grimes whose solution combines some skin in the game for Academic Institutions to the mix and thus assures that no student will ever carry debt unless the student is successful with a job in their field of study. Here is how the new loan system would work.

Nobody gets a loan unless the college or university agrees to take all of the risk of the loan. If the student is successful, she or he will pay reasonable amounts on a monthly basis. If the student is jobless, since the university vouched for the student, the school will owe all of the debt. Academic institutions are smart. They will stop lending quickly to students with very little prospects of being able to pay the loan back. If students do not maintain acceptable averages, they will be expelled, and the university will pay their balance. If they want to go to college in the future, it will be cash only. What do you think?

A Rigged System

I am confident that President Trump would re-enfranchising America's youngest generation of adults by eradicating student debt and pay the balance via savings no longer spent subsidizing illegal immigrants.

In his own words, regarding recent graduates: "They go, and they work, and they take loans, and they're borrowed up, and they can't breathe, and they get through college and the worst thing is, they go through that whole process and they don't have any job." Trump has it right. He sees how this rigged system has snuffed out the optimism of a bright generation that now gives way to cynicism and despair.

If I am elected as your Senator, I will help enact legislation that eradicates all Student Debt, effective immediately.

Boost Social Security Now

Social Security is no longer publicly discussed by our duplicitous media despite the fact that seniors' issues need the spotlight now more than ever. The media derided the implied greed of SSR recipients who received a whopping two percent cost of living raise to kick off 2018, as if oblivious to the fact that the inflation rate for 2017 was nearly 11%. Not 2%, but 11%.

No wonder seniors are struggling when their cost for purchases goes up 11% and their COLA to make up for that is a mere 2%. How do I know that, and you don't?

There are several ways Americans can investigate how much government lies cost them each year. The government purposely underestimates the cost of living to deprive our elderly of a commensurate actual increase in earned benefits. One such method for you to use is to subscribe to the Chapwood index or you may explore Shadowstats.com.

Seniors unfortunately are running out of whatever financial cushions they may ever have had, and their plight today is dire. I encourage you all to research the degree to which government deceptions are resulting in these surreptitious deprivations.

After decades being saturated by our mainstream propaganda rags, it is refreshing to finally see the truth in print. The Chapwood Index reflects the true cost-of-living increase in America. It is updated and released twice a year. There the ruses or mis-directions of the government are not included in its pages. Instead, it truthfully reports the unadjusted actual cost and price fluctuation of the top 500 items on which Americans spend their after-tax dollars in the 50 largest cities in the nation.

It exposes why middle-class Americans—salaried workers who are given routine pay hikes and retirees who depend on annual increases in their corporate pension and Social Security payments—cannot maintain their standard of living. Plainly and simply, the Index shows that their income can't keep up with their expenses and it explains why they increasingly have to turn to the government for entitlements for supplementation.

Mainstream Democrats like Senator Casey and Nancy Pelosi exacerbate the situation by allowing use of even more inequitable methods such as the new chained CPI to help assure that Seniors can languish in poverty as soon as possible.

The problem of lacking transparency on true costs (true inflation) occurs because salary and benefit increases are pegged to the fraudulent Consumer Price Index (CPI), which for more than a century has purported to reflect the fluctuation in prices for a typical "basket of goods" in American cities — but which actually hasn't done that for more than 30 years

The middle class has seen its purchasing power decline dramatically in the last three decades, forcing more and more people to seek entitlements when their savings are gone. And as long as pay raises and benefit increases are tied to a false CPI, this trend will continue.

In the past, nobody was anxious to throw the proverbial grandma under the bus. Now, believe it or not, hordes of constituencies are lining up to be the first to fleece what should belong to her into the eternal abyss, never to be seen again. The list of offenders includes: Congress, government officials, professors in academia, the "greatest" economic advisors the world has ever known, and dejected stand-alone economists who failed to gain tenure at a university.

This group of elite misfits have formed a diabolical consortium to cheat seniors out of their due cost of living increases promised from the very day the SSR act was passed by Franklin Delano Roosevelt.

As the mainstream Democrats kowtow to cultural elites and financial institutions, turning their backs on the workers and middle-class that defined their constituency for much of the 20th century, it is up to us to pick up the slack and fight for the rights of everyday Americans. When SSR was enacted, the president promised full dollar value throughout the years in order to ensure its passage in 1933. We cannot let this be undermined by the likes of Senator Casey and his allies under Chuck Schumer and Nancy Pelosi.

Many Americans are concerned that the Social Security program itself may not be able to sustain itself while others see the government cheating on the cost of living increases (CPI) thereby predetermining a life of squalor for seniors.

All successful societies throughout the ages, have maintained respect and dignity for their elders. Not only is cheating seniors a moral failure, it is a sign of a civilization entering an era of decay.

While seniors are losing their homes and many, for want of bread and milk, are on the verge of heading to the proverbial poorhouse or worse—the clutches of the Grim Reaper, Congress in 2018 pretended to care, giving a 2% raise, but then quickly snatched it right back in the dead of night via a Medicare Part B premium increase. This additional Medicare Part B charge for necessary health services for seniors was excluded from the cost of living calculations.

Thus, to pay Medicare part B, seniors are forced to use their "generous" 2% raises there, rather than to offset the costs brought forth from inflation in 2017 for which the 2% was intended. Since the real inflationary cost increases were closer to 11%, that means that instead of 9% that seniors were to endure, they accrued a full load of 11% in price increases. It's easy to understand why this constant drainage of resources is unsustainable for a senior citizen.

How did we reach this point?

Early in the administration of disgraced former President Bill Clinton, an economist named Michael Boskin, and Alan Greenspan, Chairman of the Board of Governors of the Federal Reserve System, devised a scheme that would allow for market basket "substitutions" to artificially lower the cost of living and result in lower payments to our oldest Americans. Prior to their involvement, the consumer price index (CPI) was measured using the cost of a fixed basket of goods, a fairly simple and straightforward concept.

The identical basket of goods would be priced at prevailing market costs for each period, and the period-to-period change in the cost of that market basket represented the rate of inflation in terms of maintaining a constant standard of living. That was self-evidently fair and reasonable, and predictably resulted in seniors receiving annual

COLA increases in tandem with the prices of goods actually increasing.

But Boskin and Alan Greenspan argued that when one item in the basket, for instance steak, became too expensive, the consumer would substitute hamburger for the steak, and that the inflation measure should reflect the costs tied to buying hamburger rather than the steak. Eventually, it became OK for the bureaucrats to replace hamburger with less expensive tuna and eventually because the protein value was the same, cat tuna replaced regular tuna in the market basket.

To further obscure the true cost of living, other items were selectively removed from the basket when the prices were high and then reinserted when the prices were low.

Many people have been familiar with this ruse. For example, a 1970s economic commentator named Barry Ritholtz joked that Greenspan's core inflation metric can more accurately be described as "inflation ex-inflation," meaning inflation after all of the inflation has been excluded. This demonstrates that the deception of seniors has been intentional, and it continues with a new notion called the chained CPI that will cost seniors even more.

The fact is that government has deceitfully stolen right from the pockets of our beloved seniors by denying them a fair cost of living increase. Some have even suggested that the government believes a natural limit exists on the criticism this could engender because over time, many of the complaints will be silenced by their deaths. Charming.

Walter J. Williams, an American blessing who operates the Shadowstats site has demonstrated that seniors have been stiffed by much more than just 125% and in fact should be receiving more than 4 times what their dollars were worth in 1980. That's $450 instead of $100.00. Any senior would love to have even a small proportion of that loss back.

I hope I have convinced you all that seniors have been ripped off and are being ripped off financially by their government. Congress is the real culprit.

So, what do I recommend for now? A gradual remedy. Since it would be difficult to give seniors the proper increase immediately needed to offset this quagmire caused by government malfeasance, my recommendation would be to approach it gradually, in a way that seniors would be somewhat pleased, and be able to live out their golden years in a more dignified manner.

For the next four years, the COLA boost that I'd recommend would be 15% above the real inflation rate. After four consecutive years, that should be sufficient to remove seniors from the on-deck circle they currently occupy directly outside the homeless shelter. That's all it would take.

Thank you for your attention on these important matters.

In conclusion, I must again express my gratitude for your consideration and any support as we work together to make America even greater.

God bless America and help us all make her better!

Other Books by Brian Kelly: (amazon.com, and Kindle)

It's Time for The John Doe Party… Don't you think? By By Elephants.
Great Players in Florida Gators Football… Tim Tebow and a ton of other great players
Great Coaches in Florida Gators Football… The best coaches in Gator history.
The Constitution by Hamilton, Jefferson, Madison, et al. The Real Constitution
The Constitution Companion. Will help you learn and understand the Constitution
Great Coaches in Clemson Football The best Clemson Coaches right to Dabo Sinney
Great Players in Clemson Football The best Clemson players in history
Winning Back America. America's been stolen and can be won back completely
The Founding of America… Great book to pick up a lot of great facts
Defeating America's Career Politicians. The scoundrels need to go.
Midnight Mass by Jack Lammers… You remember what it was like Hreat story
The Bike by Jack Lammers… Great heartwarming Story by Jack
Wipe Out All Student Loan Debt--Now! Watch the economy go boom!
No Free Lunch Pay Back Welfare! Why not pay it back?
Deport All Millennials Now!!! Why they deserve to be deported and/or saved
DELETE the EPA, Please! The worst decisions to hurt America
Taxation Without Representation 4th Edition Should we throw the TEA overboard again?
Four Great Political Essays by Thomas Dawson
Top Ten Political Books for 2018… Cliffnotes Version of 10 Political Books
Top Six Patriotic Books for 2018… Cliffnotes version of 6 Patriotic Boosk
Why Trump Got Elected!.. It's great to hear about a great milestone in America!
The Day the Free Press Died. Corrupt Press Lives on!
Solved (Immigration) The best solutions for 2018
Solved II (Obamacare, Social Security, Student Debt) Check it out; They're solved.
Great Moments in Pittsburgh Steelers Football… Six Super Bowls and more.
Great Players in Pittsburgh Steelers Football ,,,Chuck Noll, Bill Cowher, Mike Tomin, etc.
Great Coaches in New England Patriots Football,,, Bill Belichick the one and only plus others
Great Players in New England Patriots Football… Tom Brady, Drew Bledsoe et al.
Great Coaches in Philadelphia Eagles Football..Andy Reid, Doug Pederson & Lots more
Great Players in Philadelphia Eagles Football Great players such as Sonny Jurgenson
Great Coaches in Syracuse Football All the greats including Ben Schwartzwalder
Great Players in Syracuse Football. Highlights best players such as Jim Brown & Donovan McNabb
Millennials are People Too !!! Give US millennials help to live American Dream
Brian Kelly for the United States Senate from PA: Fresh Face for US Senate
The Candidate's Bible. Don't pray for your campaign without this bible
Rush Limbaugh's Platform for Americans… Rush will love it
Sean Hannity's Platform for Americans… Sean will love it
Donald Trump's New Platform for Americans. Make Trump unbeatable in 2020
Tariffs Are Good for America! One of the best tools a president can have
Great Coaches in Pittsburgh Steelers Football Sixteen of the best coaches ever to coach in pro football.
Great Moments in New England Patriots Football Great football moments from Boston to New England
Great Moments in Philadelphia Eagles Football. The best from the Eagles from the beginning of football.
Great Moments in Syracuse Football The great moments, coaches & players in Syracuse Football
Boost Social Security Now! Hey Buddy Can You Spare a Dime?
The Birth of American Football. From the first college game in 1869 to the last Super Bowl
Obamacare: A One-Line Repeal Congress must get this done.
A Wilkes-Barre Christmas Story A wonderful town makes Christmas all the better
A Boy, A Bike, A Train, and a Christmas Miracle A Christmas story that will melt your heart
Pay-to-Go America-First Immigration Fix
Legalizing Illegal Aliens Via Resident Visas Americans-first plan saves $Trillions. Learn how!
60 Million Illegal Aliens in America!!! A simple, America-first solution.
The Bill of Rights By Founder James Madison Refresh your knowledge of the specific rights for all
Great Players in Army Football Great Army Football played by great players..
Great Coaches in Army Football Army's coaches are all great.
Great Moments in Army Football Army Football at its best.
Great Moments in Florida Gators Football Gators Football from the start. This is the book.
Great Moments in Clemson Football CU Football at its best. This is the book.
Great Moments in Florida Gators Football Gators Football from the start. This is the book.
The Constitution Companion. A Guide to Reading and Comprehending the Constitution
The Constitution by Hamilton, Jefferson, & Madison – Big type and in English

PATERNO: The Dark Days After Win # 409. Sky began to fall within days of win # 409.
JoePa 409 Victories: Say No More! Winningest Division I-A football coach ever
American College Football: The Beginning From before day one football was played.
Great Coaches in Alabama Football Challenging the coaches of every other program!
Great Coaches in Penn State Football the Best Coaches in PSU's football program
Great Players in Penn State Football The best players in PSU's football program
Great Players in Notre Dame Football The best players in ND's football program
Great Coaches in Notre Dame Football The best coaches in any football program
Great Players in Alabama Football from Quarterbacks to offensive Linemen Greats!
Great Moments in Alabama Football AU Football from the start. This is the book.
Great Moments in Penn State Football PSU Football, start--games, coaches, players,
Great Moments in Notre Dame Football ND Football, start, games, coaches, players
Cross Country with the Parents A great trip from East Coast to West with the kids
Seniors, Social Security & the Minimum Wage. Things seniors need to know.
How to Write Your First Book and Publish It with CreateSpace
The US Immigration Fix--It's all in here. Finally, an answer.
I had a Dream IBM Could be #1 Again The title is self-explanatory
WineDiets.Com Presents The Wine Diet Learn how to lose weight while having fun.
Wilkes-Barre, PA; Return to Glory Wilkes-Barre City's return to glory
Geoffrey Parsons' Epoch... The Land of Fair Play Better than the original.
The Bill of Rights 4 Dummmies! This is the best book to learn about your rights.
Sol Bloom's Epoch ...Story of the Constitution The best book to learn the Constitution
America 4 Dummmies! All Americans should read to learn about this great country.
The Electoral College 4 Dummmies! How does it really work?
The All-Everything Machine Story about IBM's finest computer server.
ThankYou IBM! This book explains how IBM was beaten in the computer marketplace by neophytes

Brian has written 171 books in total. Other books can be found at amazon.com/author/brianwkelly

www.ingramcontent.com/pod-product-compliance
Lightning Source LLC
Chambersburg PA
CBHW050555280326
41933CB00011B/1855